GEORGE TAKEI

MY LOST FREEDOM

A Japanese American World War II Story

NAME _Takei, Hosato George_

No. _12832_

TO BE RETAINED BY PERSON
TO WHOM ISSUED

YOU ARE INSTRUCTED TO REPORT
READY TO TRAVEL ON:

Illustrated by **MICHELLE LEE**

Crown Books for Young Readers
New York

HI, I'M GEORGE TAKEI, an eighty-seven-year-old actor. I have "lived long and prospered," as we said on the sci-fi television show *Star Trek,* in which I played Hikaru Sulu. From my many years of living and acting, I have countless fond memories . . . some fantastical, some scary, and some amazing.

I have memories of soaring through the galaxy, driving a starship with a crack team of mates from a small blue planet called Earth. We were all different. We had different skin colors, different backgrounds, and different faiths. Yet we all worked together as a team, all contributing our own unique talent, knowledge, and ideas. We found our strength in our differences, ones that made our lives more interesting, more engaging, and more vibrant. As we said on *Star Trek,* "Infinite diversity in infinite combinations."

But I also have memories of when our differences became our devastation. When Japan attacked Pearl Harbor on December 7, 1941, my world turned horribly upside down. I am a Japanese American. My grandparents and my father came to America from Japan. My father spoke both English and Japanese fluently. He was American in every way except for his birthplace.

However, our two countries, the United States and Japan, were now at war with each other. America saw us as the enemy simply because we looked like the people who did the bombing. . . . We were seen as different from other Americans. This was unfair. We were Americans who had nothing to do with Pearl Harbor. Yet, we were imprisoned behind barbed wire fences.

I have a happier memory from a time before soldiers took us away to prison camps. My friend Donald had a giggly laugh and soft, curly blond hair. My hair was black and shinier. We were different, but we had fun playing together. After the soldiers came, I never saw Donald again. I write this book on the wish that my childish friendship with Donald could have grown up to have that same kind of bond I enjoyed in the future world of *Star Trek*.

Mama
at 10 years old

I am a grandson—and son—of immigrants. My father was brought to San Francisco when he was a boy by his father, a widower. My mother was born in Sacramento, California, to parents who had immigrated. Like all immigrants to America, my father and my grandparents came to this country boldly seeking a new life and opportunities.

Daddy
at 12 years old

I was just four years old when Japan bombed Pearl Harbor, on the island of Hawaii, on December 7, 1941, and the lives of all Japanese Americans were suddenly and drastically changed. The next day, President Franklin Delano Roosevelt declared war on Japan. February 19, 1942, now commemorated as the Day of Remembrance, was a day that we Japanese Americans will never forget: when the president ordered all Japanese Americans on the West Coast to be rounded up and jailed in prison camps.

It was all scary and confusing.

"FROM THE NBC NEWSROOM IN NEW YORK . . . PRESIDENT ROOSEVELT SAID IN A STATEMENT TODAY THAT THE JAPANESE HAVE ATTACKED PEARL HARBOR . . . HAWAII, FROM THE AIR. I REPEAT THAT PRESIDENT ROOSEVELT SAYS THAT THE JAPANESE HAVE ATTACKED PEARL HARBOR, IN HAWAII, FROM THE AIR."

I was grateful that Daddy took charge and Mama was brave. This is the story of how they cared for my siblings, Henry and Reiko, and me and kept us safe.

Bang, bang, bang! US Army soldiers pounded on the door. They ordered us to leave our home on Garnet Street in Los Angeles.

We took only what we could carry and were sent to Santa Anita racetrack.

Each family was assigned a horse stall to sleep in, still stinky from the stench of horse manure. Mama said it was "humiliating."

Daddy remained silent.

But I thought it would be fun to sleep where the horsies slept.

The stalls were full of creepy bugs, flying insects, and germs.
Baby Reiko was the first to get sick. Then I did too.
Our mama lovingly cared for us.

A few months later, we moved again, this time by train. I asked Daddy why.

After a while he said, "We're going on a long vacation in the country."

Two treats! A train ride AND a vacation in the country!

I thought every vacation by train had unsmiling soldiers with rifles stationed at both ends of each car.

Mama's duffel bag was the best thing about it. Whenever any of us got bored, she reached into that bag and pulled out a lollipop or a picture book or our very own water canteen.

We journeyed three days and two nights, and, finally, our train huffed through the green lushness of Arkansas to our destination: Camp Rohwer.

The soldiers walked up and down the train aisle roaring like lions. They didn't scare me at all. They sounded silly. Then one of our young men shouted, "We're approaching Camp Rohwer now." That's what the soldiers were trying to say—Rohwer! I couldn't believe *this* was our vacation place!

It was a sweltering hot late-summer day at Block 6, Barrack 2, Unit F, our new home. Before we went inside, Daddy opened the three windows and one door to "cool" the unit down. When we finally entered, a black potbellied stove greeted our sweat-drenched family. It was a cruel joke.

14

Mama placed her heavy duffel bag on top of the suitcases. "I show you something now," she stated. She reached in and lifted out a compact wooden box. She pulled on a handle. Up popped . . . her portable sewing machine!

Daddy whispered, "This was forbidden! All mechanical things with sharp points and edges were prohibited."

"I know," Mama said matter-of-factly. "But children be needing new clothes in camp."

Daddy burst out in uncontrollable laughter. Mama joined in, and Henry and I did, too, without understanding why.

Mama plunged into her new task of making a cozy dwelling for us. She found army surplus fabrics and sewed window curtains. She gathered rags, tore them into strips, and braided them into colorful rugs. She asked a kind neighbor, Mr. Yamada, to make a table and a tiny chair from scrap lumber.

Mama even made sculpture out of twisting and curving plant branches.

We on Block 6 were many kinds of people: farmers and fishermen, shopkeepers and doctors, truck drivers and schoolteachers. We were as young as baby Reiko and as old as eighty-year-old Mrs. Kato. We were a mix of Issei—immigrants—and American born—Nisei. Some were from hot, dry Arizona; some were from wet, green Oregon. Most of us were from northern, central, and southern California.

We were all so different. Yet we had one thing in common: we were all Japanese American. We needed to work together as a community. We needed a bond that would tie us together.

Daddy spoke Japanese and English fluently. So he could relate to both the immigrants and the American-born generation.

BLOCK 6

Daddy was determined not to allow the gloom, despair, and suppressed anger to take over the camp. He volunteered in all sorts of ways, delivering cots, helping in emergencies, and calming down people who were upset.

Daddy was elected block manager of Block 6 so that he could represent our issues to the camp administration.

Since baseball was popular in Block 6, Daddy suggested building a diamond. Before long, the whole block was cheering at the games.

Daddy arranged for Japanese folksong nights for the elders and dances for the teenagers.

I remember hearing the big band music of Benny Goodman and Tommy Dorsey wafting over the night air as I drifted off to sleep.

Camp Rohwer was a strange and magical place. We'd never seen trees rising out of murky waters or such colorful butterflies. Our block was surrounded by a drainage ditch, home to tiny, wiggly black fishies. I scooped them up into a jar.

One morning they had funny bumps. Then they lost their tails and their legs popped out. They turned into frogs!

But to Mama, everything in Rohwer was dangerous. "Oh abunai, so abunai," she worried.

I began kindergarten at Rohwer. As we recited "with liberty and justice for all" from the Pledge of Allegiance, I could see the fence and a sentry tower right outside my schoolhouse window. I was too young to know that those words meant the very opposite of being guarded by soldiers *in a barbed wire camp.*

One cold winter morning, I woke up and looked out on a breathtaking sight: soft, new-fallen snow. Before long, we had our first and best family snowball fight ever, a perfect way to get ready for Christmas.

On Christmas Day, we waited eagerly in the mess hall.

"Ho-ho-ho!" In waddled Santa Claus. But he looked nothing like Santa Claus. He was Japanese! A fake Japanese Santa!

I kept the secret to myself because the other kids were so happy to meet this Santa. Maybe the soldiers had kept out the real Santa?

We had been at Rohwer for a year when the government changed its mind. Now they needed our young men and women to serve in the war. But all of us Japanese Americans had been classified as "enemy aliens." How could "enemies" serve as US soldiers?

Everyone in camp over the age of seventeen had to answer a list of questions. For Daddy and Mama, those were trick questions, especially for numbers 27 and 28.

27. Are y___ ___ng to serve in the armed forces ___ of the ___

28. Will you ___ unqualified allegiance to the United St___ all attack___ ___eign or domestic forces and forswear ___ other foreign go___ ___nt, power, or organization?

(Date)

NOTE.— Any person who knowingly and willfully fal___ ___urisdiction of any department or agency of ___

Daddy and Mama both thought that the two questions were stupid. The only honest answers were "No" and "No." Those who answered yes were drafted by the government to fight for America in Europe. My parents, by answering firmly and honestly, were branded "disloyal" and forced to leave Camp Rohwer. We would be sent back across the country . . . to a harsher camp called Camp Tule Lake in northern California.

tates on com hat duty, wherever ordered?

America and faithf
n of allegiance or obedience to the Japanese emperor, or any

United States from any or

NO

NO

Camp Tule Lake was called a "segregation camp for disloyals." It was nothing like the lush and verdant swampland of Camp Rohwer.

Tule Lake was a maximum-security prison with three layers of barbed wire fences, sentry towers equipped with machine guns pointed right at us, and huge, rumbling tank patrols.

Tule Lake was the largest of the ten prison camps and held the most inmates—more than 18,000 people. Half were children like Henry, Reiko, and me.

Once again, Mama began making a cozy home out of a tar paper barrack. Daddy specially ordered linoleum for our cold, dusty floor. I loved being close to the mess hall because Henry and I could be the first in line for our meals. Poor Mama hated all the noise and the smells. "Stink terrible," she complained.

"It's a trade-off," Daddy comforted her. "Now we have two small rooms for the five of us."

There were other pluses. Movies were shown at the mess hall. For a few hours, the movies and my imagination helped me escape our narrow lives.

One afternoon Henry and I saw a shaggy black dog behind a pile of vegetable crates. He looked so hungry we convinced our cook Mr. Kikutani to give him a piece of wiener teriyaki.

The dog gobbled it up so quickly we knew he was still hungry. We took him to our unit and begged Mama for cookies.

The dog made a ruckus. But once he gave Mama a great big doggy smile, she let him stay. We had a new friend, our dog, Blackie.

We built a doghouse for him. He escorted us to school and patiently waited for us. He even made friends with Mr. Kikutani, who eventually sneaked tidbits for him after dinner.

Smart dog, that Blackie.

He made living in Tule Lake so much better.

At Tule Lake, there were young men who were seething with anger at the government for calling them "disloyal." They said, "If you're going to treat us like the enemy, well then, we'll show you what kind of enemy you have to deal with!"

Each morning, the radicals jogged around the block, chanting, "Was-shoi, was-shoi, was-shoi." Then they ran off and hid in their barracks.

One night, angry soldiers came roaring into the camp in jeeps, their rifles aimed at us. They were looking for radicals, but more often than not, innocent men were thrown in jail. I remember hearing women crying and wailing.

When I asked Daddy about the radicals, he said, "In a democracy, the people have the right to assemble and protest."

Half a world away, even more bewildering events were taking place.

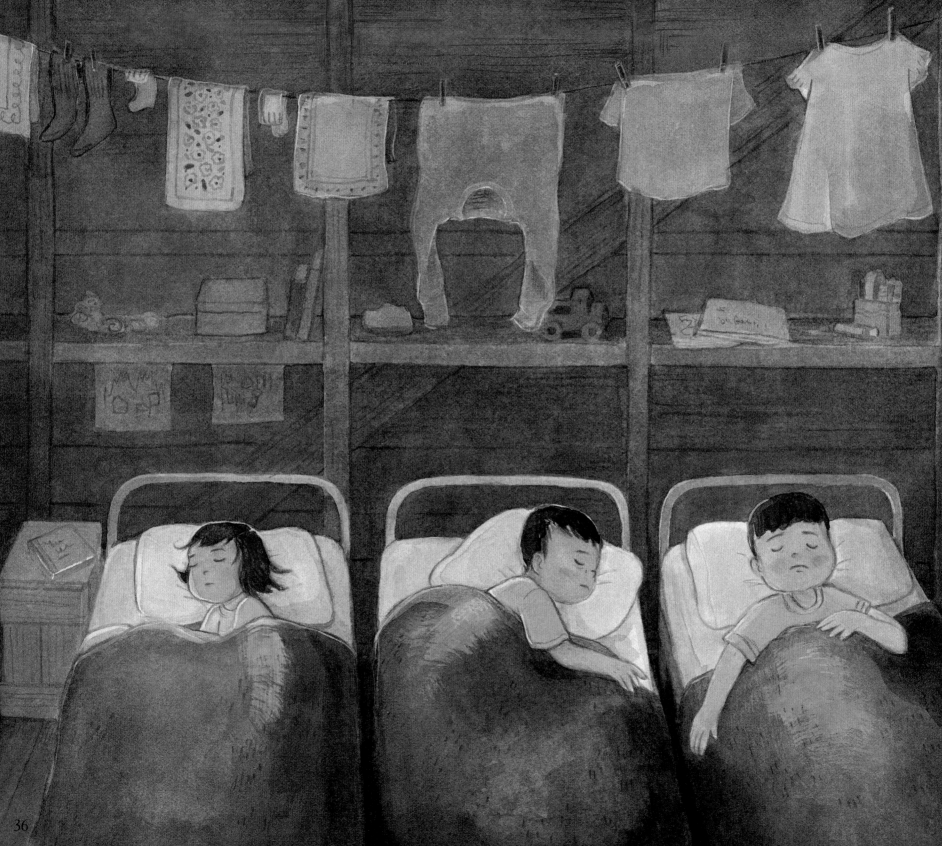

Young men who had answered "yes, yes" to questions 27 and 28—brothers and cousins of the radicals—had become US soldiers in the all–Japanese American 442nd Regimental Combat Team.

They were wearing the same uniforms as the sentry tower guards staring down at us. They were fighting heroically on far-off European battlefields carrying the American flag.

In yet another part of the world, across the Pacific, unimaginable events were taking place as well. The atomic bomb had been dropped on the Japanese cities of Hiroshima and Nagasaki. The two bombings were the most ghastly devastation the world had ever experienced.

We, imprisoned at Tule Lake, knew nothing about the bombings because newspapers and radios were forbidden. But there were vague, uncertain rumors that were painfully personal.

Mama's parents had returned to Japan . . . to Hiroshima. Mama was frantic with worry.

However, we were now adjusting to the news that the hard, terrible war was over! America was celebrating the victory. Suddenly the government was releasing us from camp as abruptly as we had been imprisoned. After four years behind barbed wire, we had nothing because the US government had taken everything.

Each of us was given twenty-five dollars and a one-way ticket to anywhere in the United States. My daddy and mama said, "Let's start all over in Los Angeles," even though they had heard that our old hometown was still hostile to Japanese Americans.

Daddy left first to find a job and a place where we could stay. After ten anxiety-filled weeks, Mama told us, "We join Daddy now in Los Angeles."

We were excited and sad at the same time. Tule Lake had become home to us. Now we were leaving our friends, our community, the rugged scenery, and our beloved Blackie.

It was a long night's train journey to Los Angeles. As the train got closer, Mama, Henry, Reiko, and I saw magnificent buildings in the sky and one soared above them all.

"That Los Angeles City Hall. Tallest building in city," said Mama. "That where Daddy and Mama married," she told us proudly.

On the platform, Henry and I shouted, "Daddy!" Our enthusiastic hugs knocked him right over.

We were all together—a family again—back in our hometown, ready to build our new future.

GLOSSARY / PRONUNCIATION GUIDE

Abunai (ah-boo-NAI): "dangerous" (p. 22)

Fumiko (FOO-me-koh): "child of treasured beauty" (p. 44)

Hiroshima (he-ROH-she-mah): "broad island." After the US dropped an atomic bomb on Hiroshima, 70,000 people died immediately, while thousands perished years later from radiation. (p. 38)

Issei (E-say): a Japanese immigrant, especially to the United States (p. 18)

Nagasaki (nah-GAH-sah-key): "long cape." The US also dropped an atomic bomb on Nagasaki, resulting in the deaths of 60,000 to 80,000 people. Citizens died from the blast and years later from radiation. (p. 38)

Nakamura (na-KAH-moo-rah): "middle village" (p. 44)

Nisei (NEE-say): American-born child of Japanese immigrants to the United States (p. 18)

Reiko (RAY-koh): "gracious child" (p. 7)

Rohwer (ROH-wer) **War Relocation Center**: Arkansas internment camp that held as many as 8,475 Japanese Americans (p. 12)

Takei (tah-KAY): "warrior well" (p. 3)

Takekuma (TAH-keh-koo-mah): "warrior" (p. 44)

Tule (TOO-lee) **Lake Segregation Center**: California internment camp that held more than 18,000 people (p. 27)

Was-shoi (wash-SHOY): a unity and peace chant (p. 34)

AUTHOR'S NOTE

My Family

Daddy, Takekuma Norman Takei, was Issei, the Japanese word for "first generation" or "immigrant." He finished his schooling, went to college, and played with the Japantown Seals baseball team in San Francisco, then moved to Los Angeles to start his dry-cleaning business. Mama, Fumiko Emily Nakamura, was Nisei, American born in Sacramento, California, but educated in Japan because of the segregated education system back then in rural California. She returned to California, where she met and married my father in Los Angeles.

I was born in Los Angeles on April 20, 1937, just three weeks before the Duke of York of England was crowned King George VI. Daddy loved all things English, and he thought it was amazing good luck that I was born just before the coronation of King George. He named me

Fumiko Emily Nakamura, on the right side of the seated man, with her family on their farm in Florin, California, circa 1920

Daddy, Mama, and baby George

after a king. So, when my brother was born a year later, he was named Henry for King Henry VIII. We are Japanese Americans named after English kings. When our sister was born two years later, that English streak of royal names was broken. She was named Nancy Reiko after a good friend of our parents. Reiko means "gracious child."

George (right, age 4) with his family before Pearl Harbor

Japanese Americans During World War II

After President Franklin Delano Roosevelt declared war on Japan, people began spitting and yelling at us on the street. We were called spies, saboteurs, and that painful word of hate: Jap! But we were Americans who had done nothing wrong; we only looked like the people who bombed Pearl Harbor. Our homes, our cars, our businesses were graffitied with venom-filled words. Weeks later, the president signed a decree classifying all Japanese Americans as "enemy aliens." It made no sense.

View of barracks at Rohwer War Relocation Center

We weren't the "enemy," and most of us were not "aliens" but born right here in the United States. Yet, orders called "curfew" came down, directing us to stay home at night and never go out. That didn't matter to us kids—we were fast asleep at night. Our parents' bank account was frozen, which meant Daddy's and Mama's money now was taken over by the government. But worse was to come. After February 19, 1942, all Japanese Americans on the West Coast were sent to ten of the bleakest and most desolate places in America—as if we were real enemies.

Rare photo of George (left, age 8), Henry, Reiko, and Mama in Tule Lake

Men of Company M, 100th Infantry Battalion, 442nd Regiment, US Fifth Army, marching through Vada, Italy, in July 1944

After the War

The end of World War II was not the end of our struggles. For us kids, the worst came after we returned to Los Angeles. We discovered that the "home" Daddy had found for us was a rundown hotel in the nastiest part of downtown Los Angeles that people called Skid Row. The building was old and falling apart. Mama said, "This a flophouse." Everything was smelly, dirty, and scary. We hated Skid Row.

Daddy's job was washing dishes at a Chinatown restaurant. Only other Asians would hire us. People returning from the camps had a hard time. So they came to Daddy, their former block manager from camp, for advice and help finding jobs. This gave Daddy the idea to open an employment office in Little Tokyo, the Japanese district downtown. I went to school in another part of Skid Row. My teacher constantly called me "the Jap boy." She was a mean old lady. I knew she hated me . . . and I hated her.

After a few months, Daddy found a dry-cleaning shop in East Los Angeles, a densely populated Mexican American neighborhood. Daddy and Mama worked long,

George (right, age 9) with his family in front of their dry-cleaning shop, 1946

hard hours and carefully saved the money they made. I went to school with Mexican American kids—"Lata," "Pelon," and "Chi-chi," whose real names were Onorato, Esteban, and Carlos. One of my favorite teachers, Mrs. Lewis, gave me my first acting role in a school Thanksgiving play as an American Indian chief. I loved going to school in East LA and making new friends. I even learned some Spanish from them.

In 1950, our parents bought a home for us in our old neighborhood in the Wilshire district. In middle school, I ran for student body president and won. At Los Angeles High School, I served as senior board president. Daddy

Henry, Reiko, and George (right, age 11) at Santa Monica Beach

was regularly advising us kids that in a participatory democracy, we all had to participate.

When I became a teenager, I was curious about growing up behind barbed wire fences. So I had many after-dinner conversations with Daddy about camp. Why were we in camp? Why didn't America's laws protect us? "They should have," Daddy said. "We live in a democracy,

George (center) was student body president of Mount Vernon Junior High School.

a government for the people. We must participate actively in the process of democracy to achieve equal justice for all and to keep terrible things from happening. We have a duty to be the people who give democracy its meaning

and its worth. As an American, I have American responsibilities."

When I became an adult, a movement began in the Japanese American community to obtain an apology and amends for the mistakes the government made so many years ago when I was a boy. Congress created a commission to gather information on the imprisonment of innocent Japanese Americans. In 1981, it held hearings. I testified at one of those hearings, sharing my boyhood memories of camp. I also told the commission that I am an American and have the same concerns about the integrity of our democracy as the commissioners. I stated:

"I believe that America is confident and strong enough to recognize a grievous failure. I believe that it is honest enough to acknowledge that damage was done. And I would like to think that it is honorable enough to provide proper restitution for the injury that was done. For in a larger sense, injury was done to those very ideals we hold as fundamental to our American system. We, all of us as Americans, must strive to redeem those precepts that faltered years ago when I was a boy. And in that role as an American, I urge restitution for the incarceration of American citizens of Japanese ancestry, because that restitution would, at the same time, be a bold move to strengthen the integrity of America."

In 1988, President Ronald Reagan signed the Civil Liberties Act on behalf of the people of the United States and officially apologized for the internment and paid redress.

However, my father had passed nine years before the apology, at age seventy-six, in 1979. It would have meant so much to him to know that America had apologized. But Mama heard the apology. She was deeply moved and told me that Daddy knew this day would come.

My childhood behind barbed wire was a mix of both fond and terrifying memories. But through it all, Mama and Daddy always took a stand. They were my solid American heroes.

To Daddy and Mama
—G.T.

For Mom and Dad
—M.L.

*Mama with Henry (age 1) and
George (right, age 2)*

*Daddy with Henry (age 2) and
George (right, age 3) before Pearl Harbor*

*Henry, Reiko, and George (right, age 16) in front of
their house*

Text copyright © 2024 by George Takei
Jacket art and interior illustrations copyright © 2024 by Michelle Lee
Family photos courtesy of George Takei

Archival Photo Credits:
Page 45: Courtesy National Archives, photo no. 537380
Page 46: Courtesy National Archives, photo no. 100310607

Visit us on the Web! rhcbooks.com
Educators and librarians, for a variety of teaching tools, visit us at RHTeachersLibrarians.com

Library of Congress Cataloging-in-Publication Data is available upon request.
ISBN 978-0-593-56635-0 (trade) — ISBN 978-0-593-56636-7 (lib. bdg.) —
ISBN 978-0-593-56637-4 (ebook)

The text of this book is set in 15-point Granjon LT Roman.
The illustrations were created using watercolor, gouache, colored pencils, and digital media.
Book design by Nicole de las Heras

MANUFACTURED IN CHINA   10 9 8 7 6 5 4 3 2 1   First Edition